TRANSITIONS

*Grace to Navigate the
Storms of Change*

Joseph Jones

Transitions
Grace to Navigate the Storms of Change
ISBN 0-88144-338-7
Copyright © 2009 by Joseph Jones

Printed by
Thorncrown Publishing
A Division of Yorkshire Publishing Group
7707 East 111th Street South, Suite 104
Tulsa, Oklahoma 74133
www.yorkshirepublishing.com

I would like to dedicate this book to the wonderful
people of The Landing Community Church
who have inspired me and encouraged me
to keep turning my dreams2destiny.

To my Tuesday night men's roundtable
where ideas are shared and dreams are born.
The ride is only beginning!

To my Mom and Dad and my brother John and
sister Jen who listened when no one else would
and who gave when no one else could

To my great kids, Brandon, Justin and Jordan
who love me unconditionally and give me the
opportunity to learn and grow every day.

To my Lord and Savior who has walked through
every transition with me and strengthened me
to keep on going when I felt like quitting.

"Forgetting what is behind and straining
towards what is ahead…"

Introduction

There are so many reasons that I wanted to write this book. One of them is found right there in the center of that word, transitions. Do you see it? Right there in the middle of transitions... it is **"I"**! That's right! "I" am <u>always</u> going through some type of transition. Yes, it's about me! It's up close and personal. My last book was all about how my life was divinely guided through many wonderful experiences in the contemporary Christian music business. As that book ended, I was "transitioning" into another career as the pastor of a church I founded in Oklahoma. Within that transition were several others and many of them surprised me and challenged me. I was learning every day how to not only survive, but how to get stronger in the midst of the challenges.

I never knew that writing books would be such a continuous process of exploration and discovery and change. I have truly engaged in the process of learning how to turn a setback into a comeback. I have juggled some very uncomfortable seasons of confusion and idleness. And when I finally do cross over in one area, another transition is waiting for me! Another reason that I wrote this book was because of what I saw when I became a pastor in 2002. I found myself surrounded by people that were also going through transitions. Most of them knew in fact that they were in a transition but they had many questions about what to do while they were there and how to act until they found themselves on the other side.

What I began to realize was that these seasons of transition that I was witnessing and experiencing never stopped. Someone was always going through one. As I ministered every week to hundreds of people, I saw a need for more in-depth dialogue about how we feel in transitions, how we move through them, and how God can make these changes into some of the most incredible moments of our lives. I even asked some of the folks that I knew to help and share their transition stories. Throughout this book you will find their stories in their own words which they have allowed me to pass on to you.

Life is programmed to change. I heard it said that life is like a river. It is moving and changing and will only start to stink when it becomes a stagnant pond. So I wanted to write this book to help us stop stinking and start thinking. Perhaps reprogram that stinkin' thinkin' and move into a better place where we are operating at our fullest potential.

Part of the learning process is becoming vulnerable and transparent. It's time for each of us to be very sincere and genuine. People are looking for real help to their real problems. As I have invested my life and told my story to others, it has helped many people to gain strength and tell their story. And that is the ingredient of true evangelism: shared experiences. This book contains many of the discoveries that showed up as my friends and family explored our lives together and found God in the middle of each and every transition.

Whether you are in a transition now, coming through one or getting ready to go into one, our prayer is that you will learn the lesson that lies in the middle of the journey to the other side of change and that you will grab that grace that Christ offers to help you navigate your trip. It can be one of the most tremendous times of personal growth you've ever had.

Godspeed!

Chapter 1

There are a variety of events that occur in our lives that will lead us into seasons of transition. The definition means **to move from one position or state to another.** It is the passage from one season into the next. It's how we cross over from one side to the other. It is the place sandwiched in between an ending and a beginning. Let me name a few...

- Single to married, married to single again (divorced)

- Divorced to remarried, working to unemployed, moving from one job to another ,going to war, coming home from war ; relocation, the loss of a loved one(grief), the birth of a new one, terminal illness(confusion)

- changing schools ; leaving school

- blending families, changing careers, retiring

- re-firing...ok, you get the picture!

TRANSITIONS

The fact of the matter is that this transition process began the moment you did! Think about your experience in leaving the womb and entering the world. You did not ask to have that happen at that particular time. God set it up. You may have done some kicking and punching during that period but God was in control. He put a nine month timetable together that may not be etched in stone, but gives us a good idea of how long it takes to "get it together". After that **designated** time period, the process pushed you out. It was due season. It was **your** moment and the first thing that happened when you were pushed out is that you got slapped! Right there on your tiny behind! In the old days some of us were even turned upside down! And it did not stop there. You screamed for a moment and then they shoved this suction thing into your nose and mouth like they wanted to suck the brain out of your head. Like a new product on an assembly line you were being made ready for your purpose. After they rubbed you raw like they were wiping syrup off a dirty table, they put you under a hot light like a packet of fries at McDonalds. When the time was right, or maybe when you were the right temperature and all looked well, they put you in a plastic container and rolled you down a bright hall. They even graded your appearance! Many things were happening around you but you had no idea what they were. Your eyes were still glued shut and the sounds were similar to what you heard before only louder. And then, finally, the chaos became calm, the brightness dimmed and you were placed in the arms of your mother. Nothing else mattered, you felt secure and peaceful. The transition from the womb to your mothers' arms was not easy but you made it. I want you to hear that. It was messy, it may not have been the prettiest thing, it was very traumatic but **YOU MADE IT!** Know that in every season of transition, <u>you will make it</u>. As you read through these pages, life will continue to happen. I do not want you to quit. I want you to endure every transitional experience and learn every beautiful lesson.

It was Dr. Edwin Louis Cole that said the way we leave one season or place determines the way we enter the next one. If I run out of the living room, I am running into the kitchen. When I leave the bedroom, I enter the bathroom. When I step out of the car, I am stepping into the parking lot at work. What we have to begin to realize is that the attitude and mentality we have when we leave one season will travel with us as we go into the next one unless we have allowed the process of transition to "reset" our hard drive.

Say this to yourself:

I am in a transitional season.

I am learning more and more about ME each day.

It's ALL Good!

God is mixing ALL of this together for MY benefit.

I will make it through!

Chapter 2

I used to be an early adopter when it came to the latest and greatest gadgets. An early adopter is the person that goes out and pays the highest retail price for the latest technology because they have to have it first. One of my adopted gadgets was the Palm Pilot. I loved it! I began to store every note, every phone number and every appointment I had in the "palm" in my little hand. It was so convenient and I felt so technologically savvy! I was as they say, "connected" and way ahead of the curve. I even downloaded a copy of the Bible to mine so I no longer needed to carry the big leather bound version anymore. I had condensed my life and simplified everything.

Then, as quickly as a sunny sky can turn to gray, as quickly as a carton of milk can go bad, a storm hit. My connection collapsed. My electronic life planner froze! That's right, it was as tightly shut up as the city of Jericho, nothing went in and nothing came out! I began to freak out because without my palm pilot I did not know when my next appointment was. Without my palm pilot I did not know the direct number for Domino's delivery! How would I read my morning devotions? What is my mission in life? It's all in my Palm Pilot! My life was crashing hard!

I searched for the box that my device came in and found the manufacturers instructions. As I began to read through the pamphlet which was 30 pages long and printed in 26 different languages, I noticed that the manufacturer had prepared for this particular problem. The directions said that if the device should ever "freeze up", simply turn it over, find this small pin hole on the back and push a paper clip or pen tip in to reset the device. It was called a <u>master reset</u>. I immediately found a paper clip and followed the instructions. And in a matter of seconds, the unit shut off and powered back up again, unfrozen, fully loaded and putting me back on the fast track again.

I think that life can have these moments too. Circumstances and situations have a way of causing us to freeze up emotionally and mentally. My personal "freeze" came in the midst of divorce. As a Christian and someone who said I do forever, I never thought I'd see that transition so I was completely unprepared. When my partner decided that she no longer wanted to be married to me I locked up. Nothing came in and nothing went out. We had a beautiful home, three incredible kids and we were the perfect family, so blessed in many ways. But God gave each of us the ability to choose what we want and I had no control over choices she was making. Just like my palm pilot, I lost my contacts, my appointments and everything that had been saved up until that time. I went through countless emotions and a variety of mind games. I began to doubt my calling as a minister. I was scared to engage in conversations with people that I did not know. To be honest I felt dirty, condemned and confused. I needed help. And in the same way I unlocked my palm pilot, I unlocked my life. I went back to the directions. I kept reading my Bible, finding different translations that said to me what I needed to hear in a way that I could understand it. I found the right words and began to notice that my manufacturer had prepared for things like divorce. I read as much as I could contain in my head and I began to notice that there was a bigger picture that I was not seeing because I "froze up". It was God who was able to turn me around, push the right button and give me the chance to reboot and be productive again. You could say that the Master reset me!

The first thing that happened was that He shut me off. He powered me down so that I could not damage myself any longer. Remember that nothing was coming in and nothing was going out. You may have to cease from some activity for a season as God begins to put you in the right position to be "reset". On my Palm Pilot there was a tool(paper clip) that was necessary to reach into the spot where the initiator button for the reset is located. The word of God, the Bible is living and active and sharper than any two-edged sword. Whatever has been able to cut into you can be cut out by the Word of God. He began to heal the hurtful words that had been spoken with healing words. His Word was the tool that I needed to begin to initiate the reset process.

Transitions will happen to all of us and rather than stay frozen and locked up we need to allow ourselves some time to do this master reset. I cannot determine when your button will be pushed but God has a way of getting the right people, the right friends and the right opportunities to you. I encourage you to talk to him, to pray. If you have never really prayed before, I want you to know that it's as easy as talking to someone you know. Jeremiah 33:3 tells us that we will call on God and He will answer. He won't just answer; he will show us some great things that we may never had imagined were possible.

Whether you coming out of a divorce, entering into a marriage, holding your first child or starting a life of sobriety, you can make it! There is hope and a future and the world is waiting for you...the new you...the healed you...the stronger you! It's ok that you may have frozen up. Everyone does. The good news is that there is someone who knows how to reset you. Go back to the directions and find out what you were made for. Let God find your reset button and let's get through this together!

Chapter 3

Change...whether we are impacted by change that we cause or change that is forced upon us, we must learn how to navigate the transition and get ourselves to a place of health, a place of wholeness. You cannot win if you do not begin. See that word in the middle of **"change"**: between the C and the E... HANG. Don't let change hang you up!

The advice that most people give us when we are going through transitions is simple...they say, "you need to move on". Well duh! I could have paid cash for a new home if I had a dollar for every time someone gave me that counsel. I already know that...but can't you see, I'm in transition! I'm not stupid! The struggle is that we have to figure out how we are to do that. The secret may lie in something I already pointed out...how we leave one position/relationship/job will determine how we enter the next. In other words, we have to not only tie up loose ends in what we are leaving, we need to package them up and ship them out to that place that memories go. If the memories are good ones, we may store them close to home so we can journey back in our mind from time to time. If the memories are bad ones, maybe that sea where Jesus casts all of our sins, called the Sea of Forgetfulness is the best spot. Remember, yesterday ended last night! I know that the reason that you are reading this book is because you do want to "move on" or at the least, "move through" this hallway of transition. I call it a hallway because for me, that is what it feels like. I already left one doorway and now it has closed behind me. But the new door has not yet opened up so here I am, in what we may call "limbo", waiting for some indicator as to where to go next. It's as uncomfortable as being in the lobby of a busy hotel with a tuxedo on because you are in a wedding. Everyone is looking at you! Everyone goes past you wondering why you are standing there because you do not look like you belong there. In other words, you aren't dressed for where you are, you are dressed for where you are going! You have been outfitted for what is coming up and yes, you don't fit where you are. But that's OK...someone who has watched you enter the hall knows where you are going. Remember God is in control. Traffic moves through the hallway but nobody just sits there. That is why this transition time seems so uncomfortable. Everyone else is on their way to someone or someplace but we don't have that information yet.

Imagine being in a beautiful hotel and having a five star suite and being locked out of your room because you misplaced your key. Would you just sit there in the hallway and cry about the fact that your key is missing or would you take the initiative and go get another key?

It is evident to me that you are not a hallway crier. You are not going to sit in the hall with last nights room service trays and complain. You will go and get another key...a key that will get you into your room. Transition isn't easy but all of us are in one, have just crossed one or are facing one. So finding our personal key is what we need. Your key may be different than mine. Your doorway of opportunity is for YOU. Sometimes the hallway isn't so miserable. That is, if you feel like the Lord is with you there!

Chapter 4

Mark 4:35 That day when evening came, he said to his disciples, "Let us go over to the other side." [36]Leaving the crowd behind, they took him along, just as he was, in the boat. There were also other boats with him. [37]A furious squall came up, and the waves broke over the boat, so that it was nearly swamped. [38]Jesus was in the stern, sleeping on a cushion. The disciples woke him and said to him, "Teacher, don't you care if we drown?"

[39]He got up, rebuked the wind and said to the waves, "Quiet! Be still!" Then the wind died down and it was completely calm.

[40]He said to his disciples, "Why are you so afraid? Do you still have no faith?"

[41]They were terrified and asked each other, "Who is this? Even the wind and the waves obey him!"

This IS a story about transition. Seems that the day of taking care of people was nearly completed and Jesus told those closest to him, the disciples, to go over to the other side. The bible said that evening had come when he said this. That is what makes transitions so ominous. Most of the time it feels that we are sent into a life change and surrounded by darkness. I am sure the disciples asked Jesus why now? Why couldn't we have gone across the lake during the day? It would have been easier; it would have been much more fun. It's easier to go to the other side when you can see it!

But a life lesson was unfolding. When we know all of the answers, when we can see all of the destination points, there is no reason to utilize faith. And we know that without faith it is impossible to please God. God was increasing their faith by exposing them to a chance to use it. I know, that sounds weird. But I doubt that the Holy Spirit said, hey, let's have some fun. Let's send them out on the ocean in the middle of the night and send a storm to really mess them up! Let's teach em' something! <u>Faith is what you use when you stop thinking about it</u>. Faith is what you will use to take the first step from where you were to where you are going. Faith steps out on nothing and finds that God put something there. It's talking about what you want to see happen next, before it happens, and talking as if it is already taking place.

I can imagine the conversation that took place. Jesus, what's wrong with this side? We are comfortable here. Everything seems to be going okay, why the change? We know where all the restaurants are, we know how many miles it is to where we want to go...we know nothing about this "other side".

Part of my healing process was to stop looking at what everyone else needed from me and start listening to what God was teaching me. To go from being married for 20 years to being "single again" with three children was a new thing. Suddenly I was trying to discern what I liked to do. I honestly did not know! I began to realize that I had not made a decision based on what I wanted for a long time. I did not know how to be me. I was scared at first because I was no longer defining myself by those that were attached to me. I was defining myself by who I was attached to. And in those transition moments(years) I had no one to speak with. No one to share my heart with. It seemed people only wanted to know details about what happened and I was left with no direction for where to go.

So I talked to the only person I could. I hooked up with the Lord because He had always been consistent. He had never let me down and though I did not know Him as well as I do now, the new intensity in our relationship was just what I needed.

He began taking me on a journey, at night, to the other side. I was going to go into a place I had never been before and I was going to have to "feel" my way. I would have thoughts I never had before, see things I had never noticed. Life would change for my children and I would have to walk with them through their personal transitions. Without God I had no clue. Realizing that you do not have all the answers and being ok with that will help. You are in a new discovery mode and as you dig deep into YOU and how you are put together, you will realize just how special you are. I began to understand that God may care more about the individuals that get married than the institution of marriage. He loved me. He loved my spouse. And we would go through some transitions that had to be experienced. I had to "feel" the way. I had felt discarded, abandoned and betrayed and I was being held captive by those emotions. But the past was over. I couldn't change it. And the only way the past could poison my future was if I invited it into my present. I decided not to send that invitation. I did what the disciples did that day when evening had come. I listened to Jesus and I got into the boat and began to row to the other side.

Chapter 5

I wasn't a Christian long before I began to see that it was not always "blue skies smiling at me". I asked the Lord to come and live in my heart in November of 1977 in a dorm room at a secular university. I wanted to be that new creation that the Bible talks about in 2 Corinthians 5:17. I wanted the old things out and the new stuff to show up and I wanted that to happen NOW! I transferred to a Christian university knowing that if I was in a good and clean environment I could live a 'saved" life. As soon as I landed in my new "saved" environment, I noticed that most of the kids on my dorm floor weren't even saved. They were at Christian college because their parents had sent them, not because they wanted to be there. So they lived one way and talked another. That was a storm in my spiritual life. Because I was such a young and immature believer, I started to become like my environment rather than allowing my new relationship with Christ to change it. You could say I became a thermometer rather than a thermostat. A thermostat can control the temperature but a thermometer can only tell you what the temperature is. I was living a lie most of the time and felt sick about it.

When the disciples took that midnight boat ride across the lake, the Bible says they too found themselves in a storm. In the Bible it was called a furious squall. Guess that anytime you start to move in the right direction you might just as well prepare yourself for a bit of bad weather. Seems that anytime I have moved forward in God the winds of adversity always rise up against me. Guess it is the devil's way to get you to quit. It's like he is saying, "Stop moving forward in the direction that God is calling you." Now let me give you a word of caution here. If you stop moving forward, you're dead in the water! Waves will come, water may even start to make your life feel as though it is sinking. But you must keep rowing.

While the disciples were struggling with these adverse weather conditions, Jesus was sleeping quietly on the boat. Yes, that's right. The same boat that is freaking out all of the disciples. They ran in to wake him up..."don't you care about what is happening? Can't you see what we are all going through? Perhaps Jesus knew something that they had not yet learned. This contrary wind, these crashing waves are not going to stop our progress. You could say that he didn't lose any sleep over it. He was resting in the midst of the storm. He was gaining His strength in the midst of the storm. You see, there is something that you are being prepared for even during this transition. God develops our character in the midst of adversity. Our personality begins to be shaped. We gain strength and we gain wisdom. We start to learn many things about ourselves. And we also learn many things about those in the boat with us. It's in that adversity that our weaknesses are exposed. Not exposed so that we can criticize them. Exposed so that we can begin to strengthen them and become healthy and whole again.

That furious squall was not going to last forever. It had a purpose and when that purpose was fulfilled, it ended. The chaos turned calm again. And you know what made all the difference? The difference was Jesus.

In the middle of one of my trips to the other side I found there were times when I was raising my voice at the Lord..."why did this happen to me?" "Don't you care about my family?" Can't you see this storm? Yet as the waves crashed into my life and the winds howled, I kept trying to hear His voice. At first it was faint and distant. But the more intently I listened, the more audible it became and I started to learn His lesson. The most painful times are those times when you can only see your problems and not the solution. The Bible says to "fix your eyes on Jesus, the author and the finisher of your faith". When we can start <u>looking</u> at Him we can start <u>leaning</u> on Him. And when we start helping to row the boat we have less time to rock it. You will get to the other side. The disciples did. They made it through the rain. And you will too!

Chapter 6

Hearing the Lord's voice in the midst of "crossing over" is so important. When you feel isolated and shut off from the world that used to be you, the voices that speak out to you do not stop. People will always have opinions and many times they will say things off the top of their heads without knowing how those words will impact you. In the Book of Matthew there is another lake encounter which speaks about Jesus walking out on the water in the middle of the night towards the boat. He wasn't in the boat, he was on the water! I must confess that many of the transitions I have gone through have felt more like this account because I really did not feel like God was right there in the storm with me. At least not at first.

> Matt 14:22 Immediately Jesus made the disciples get into the boat and go on ahead of him to the other side, while he dismissed the crowd. 23After he had dismissed them, he went up on a mountainside by himself to pray. When evening came,

he was there alone, [24]but the boat was already a considerable distance from land, buffeted by the waves because the wind was against it.

[25]During the fourth watch of the night Jesus went out to them, walking on the lake. [26]When the disciples saw him walking on the lake, they were terrified. "It's a ghost," they said, and cried out in fear.

[27]But Jesus immediately said to them: "Take courage! It is I. Don't be afraid."

[28]"Lord, if it's you," Peter replied, "tell me to come to you on the water."

[29]"Come," he said.

Then Peter got down out of the boat, walked on the water and came toward Jesus. [30]But when he saw the wind, he was afraid and, beginning to sink, cried out, "Lord, save me!"

[31]Immediately Jesus reached out his hand and caught him. "You of little faith," he said, "why did you doubt?"

[32]And when they climbed into the boat, the wind died down. [33]Then those who were in the boat worshiped him, saying, "Truly you are the Son of God."

During the fourth watch, sometime between 3 and 6 am, right in the middle of that storm, Jesus comes toward the boat. The disciples see this figure on top of the water and they scream in terror because they cannot tell who it is. Jesus spoke and assured them that it was all right. He said I am here, don't be afraid. There was a disciple in the boat that was known for his boldness and brazenness. His name was Peter. Peter is that guy who is not afraid to say what he feels. He's that guy who often hurts your feelings because he is so brutally honest and callous in his presentation. He has passion and wears all of his emotions on his sleeve. And if you try to take the Lord out of his life, he'll cut your ear off!

When the voice of Jesus was heard, Peter said, "Lord, if it's really you, tell me to come." Think about what Peter was really saying. Lord, I can't see you but I have heard that voice before. And though I cannot SEE you in the middle of this storm, I can HEAR your voice and I want you to keep speaking so that I can move in the direction of that voice. For me the hardest part of enduring transitions is the ability to distinguish all of the voices and find a way to get to Jesus' voice. Every time that I would find a place to vent as I went through divorce, the sea of emotions and adversity would rise up again. If you have ever put lighter fluid on a fire that was just starting, you know what can happen when you start venting and everyone starts throwing in their opinions and comments. You get a fire that blazes out of control! For me every song on the radio took me back to the shoreline. Every place that we would eat together as a family made me stop rowing. And every time that I allowed these voices to access my life, all I wanted to do was splash and scream.

I am not sure when that moment arrives where you finally are able to tune into God's voice. It was the fourth watch in our story when Jesus came which is somewhere between 3 and 6am. There may be a few watches that occur before you "feel" His presence. Perhaps it's like finding a good radio station in your car and you just have to keep changing the frequencies until you land on the one that is clear to you. Or maybe you have to drive to a different spot in town before it becomes clearer. I imagine that I have this divine GPS system in me and when I am in sight of the signal, I get reception and all is well. When the satellite has direct access to me, everything is crystal clear. So I try to keep all of the obstacles from getting between me and the Lord. Sometimes I can control that, other times life seems to interfere. Peter said, "Lord, if that's really you, tell me to come to where you are".

Where He is, well, that's where you and I need to be. I can't see you but I can hear your voice and if you will just keep talking, I'm going to get up and get out of this boat and walk toward you. It's that moment when you no longer hear the crashing waves or the screams of terror...just the still small voice of God that says "keep coming". And that is the only voice that will empower you to get up and take a step out on top of the water. I believe that Jesus said more than what the Bible tells us. Peter needed to listen and the Lord needed to keep talking. You know those ads on television for those different pills that will help your symptoms but there are some side effects that they say as a disclaimer and they speak about 100 miles per hour at the end of the commercial? Peter was probably like you and me...excited about the Lord speaking and when Jesus said come he jumped out and started walking! Imagine that he missed the Lord saying, "Come...and when you come keep walking towards my voice...failure to listen may cause you to begin to sink which may lead to an underwater death!

I know you may never have heard the story like that before but that is the way I think. Peter steps out of the boat and starts to walk on top of the waves that were trying to capsize him! What was in him that day is also in you and me. We've got to listen to the right voices and then use our faith to walk on top of the things that tried to stop our progress. More than ever before I believe that what doesn't kill you will make you stronger. Peter used the adversity to make a connection and get to Christ. It may feel like you are in a foreign land and that nobody speaks your language. If you look real closely you can see the shadow...is it Jesus? Listen. Is that really you Jesus? Tell me to come. And Jesus says, come. Whether you get up and get out of the boat will be your decision.

As I mentioned already, I received many stories from people that I know, which I want to share with you so that you can see how different folks handle the seasons of transition. The first one is from my mom...

"One of the most difficult transitions that I've found in my life was becoming an "empty nester". When my first child, Joe, left home for college, it was a strange feeling – like part of me was missing. But then I still had two children at home and I didn't have time to dwell on my own sense of loss.

TRANSITIONS

I wrote him letters and we called and I stayed in close contact with him. Six years later my daughter Jennifer left for college. Again that pull to a mother's heart – my child was gone – but still there was one more at home. As with all the others, this one, John, was involved in many things and so was I, so time was filled and I was still very busy. The bombshell came two years later when the third child left. The hole in my heart was now huge!! No children left at home! My husband and I both felt a loss but somehow I think it's very different for moms. I would go into the bedrooms to clean and I would cry.....cooking for two I would cry...doing laundry for two brought sadness. I didn't want my children to return because my job was to raise them to be independent strong people and I believed I had done that.

However, that didn't change the way I felt. Then one day I had a call from a friend who had been listening to me as I unsuccessfully tried to explain my feelings to her. She told me about a book she had seen that she would be sending to me. It was called "The Kids Are All Gone, Lord, But I'm Still Here." When I read it, it was an amazing lift to my heart. The author was able to put into words everything I had experienced but couldn't relate to my husband or anyone else. I have since shared that book with many others and it is now out of print and I believe it has been for a very long time. It surely helped me make a transition from sadness to acceptance and begin a new chapter in my life."

"Jean Jones: My Sweet Mother!"

Chapter 7

I have made some references to the Bible in the previous chapters. There is another story that includes boats and getting out of our comfort zone or self-pity area and moving towards the next season.

LUKE 5:1 One day as Jesus was standing by the Lake of Gennesaret, with the people crowding around him and listening to the word of God, ²he saw at the water's edge two boats, left there by the fishermen, who were washing their nets. ³He got into one of the boats, the one belonging to Simon, and asked him to put out a little from shore. Then he sat down and taught the people from the boat.

⁴When he had finished speaking, he said to Simon, "Put out into deep water, and let down the nets for a catch."

⁵Simon answered, "Master, we've worked hard all night and haven't caught anything. But because you say so, I will let down the nets."

⁶When they had done so, they caught such a large number of fish that their nets began to break. ⁷So they signaled their partners in the other boat to

come and help them, and they came and filled both boats so full that they began to sink.

⁸When Simon Peter saw this, he fell at Jesus' knees and said, "Go away from me, Lord; I am a sinful man!" ⁹For he and all his companions were astonished at the catch of fish they had taken, ¹⁰and so were James and John, the sons of Zebedee, Simon's partners.

Then Jesus said to Simon, "Don't be afraid; from now on you will catch men." ¹¹So they pulled their boats up on shore, left everything and followed him.

I am a huge fan of dreaming about the impossible. I like to shoot for the stars and things that others would say cannot be done. In my first career in contemporary Christian music that is what I did. I was hooked up with another dreamer and when two or more are gathered together in God's world, stuff happens! Good stuff! Great stuff! In 20 years of working in music ministry I produced over 1000 live events and saw more than a million people accept Christ into their lives. That's more than a million folks that would enjoy the wonderful feeling of being saved and then at some point the wonderful letdown of feeling prisoner again! That's right...being a fully devoted follower of Christ is not a cheap easy way to get through life. Storms of life fall on believers and non-believers. Chances are you will not always be strong and invincible. In fact, I would bet that ALL of these people that I witnessed receiving Christ were going to go through some seasons of transition. Even those closest to Christ when he walked on this earth found out that just because He was close didn't mean that trouble stayed away from you. You don't always catch fish just because you have a pole and some bait. Again, we can look at Peter and see that.

Peter was the Jimmy Houston of the day, without the sunglasses! He may not have had all of the gadgets that we have today but there is one thing that was certain, Peter knew how to catch fish. In the story above we see that the fisherman had been out all night, doing what they were good at doing and they came back with nothing. They were tired, frustrated, and disappointed. It's the way you may feel when you leave a job or a city. It's the way I left high school. Don't get me wrong, I got all that I could out of high school. I began to recognize the gifts that God had planted in me and I even started to use them. Proverbs 18:16 tells us that a man's gift will take him before great men. I was looking for all of that. I was voted most likely to succeed because of my love for music and the arts. But now high school was over. I was tired because I had worked very hard. I was frustrated because now I would have to leave something that I had learned so well. And I was disappointed because I knew that where I was going was not going to be like where I was.

Peter and the rest of the fisherman were busy putting away the tools of the trade because to them, the fishing time was over. They had been out all night and caught nothing. I am certain that in the state of mind that they were in, their attitudes may not have been admirable. Jesus sees a boat sitting on the waters edge and asks them to push it into the water. The crowd that had gathered to hear his teaching was growing and he was going to preach from the boat. But there were several other lessons that he was weaving through this story. He wanted Peter to keep fishing. He wanted Peter to fish differently than before.

Now Peter's reaction to moving on may be like ours. Lord, I've been there, done it and bought the t-shirt. I have fished all I can get out of this lake. Jesus asked Peter to go deeper. What? Go to a part of the lake that you would never have gone to and let the nets down again. What Peter did not realize was that Jesus had already prepared the way. He had already gotten the boat back into the water. If you are going to move through transitions you have to get the boat back into the water. Get back in the game, put on your uniform and take the field.

Jesus told Peter to "Launch out to the deep". Now the avid fisherman knows that this is not the best time to fish. And the deep is surely not the best place to fish at this time of day. And the waters that we are being asked to go into we have never been to...they are uncharted. Unfamiliar territory is always hard to navigate. There are no recognizable landmarks or personal milestones. It's a new day and there are new places that God is ready to direct us to. You may have thought that the time invested in your previous season was wasted. You feel that way because you don't know where you are going yet. You still do not see the value of the lessons that you have already learned that will serve you where you are going. You are not aware that Jesus already has your boat back in the water and all he wants you to do is what you are good at doing. He is taking you across...from one position to another.

Notice that Peter really isn't overwhelmingly in favor of this idea. But he respects the one that is giving the directions. Maybe this is where you are right now with that new job. You're being asked to step up and into an area that you have never been in before. You are hesitant, maybe even a bit nervous and you may be slow in making decisions because you don't want to fail. Peter thought that they had all failed. He thought he was done. He was putting the nets away as Jesus was getting things in order for him to use them again. Jesus wanted to give him a new perspective on fishing. Jesus wanted to take him places that he'd never dreamed of. Jesus wanted to give him some new nets!

The transition that you are in right now is not new. If everything feels good, go with the momentum of that change. If you are like Peter and reluctantly agreeing to move because you hear the voice of the Lord calling out, know that this is a set up. You are being set up for a wonderful surprise! Peter was too!

Another TRANSITION Story...

"I'm coming up on my 8th year of finding out that I had a brain tumor. Most people that have a brain tumor don't survive this long. Then why me? I often wrestle the "why". Is this a test from God? Or was it to deliver me from Satan's scare. Satan tried

to get me from going against God, by messing with my mind, literally (brain tumor). I have a lot of time on my hands now. I lost everything, my whole right side is affected, I am unemployable because I can't drive, even lost my ability to ride my mountain bike, golf, and speak effectively, plus a whole lot more.

I thank God for my family who has to take care me. I thank God for "Landing" me here where Pastor Joe has taught me that there are seasons in my life. I believe I survived because God has the master plan, what it is he hasn't revealed to me yet. Many people have laid hands on me, and prayed for me. I believe there is a reason why the Lord hasn't restored my body yet, someone has not been touched in one way or another. I believe that the Lord has already healed my soul. How long is this season going to last? As long as it takes! I believe that God, Jesus and the Holy Ghost, will get me there.

Lord, forgive me for only thinking of myself using the "I" word too often.

Lord, forgive me for my impatience for healing me in your own time Amen.

Behold, I make all things new. Rev. 21:5"

"Jim Cover"

Chapter 8

As a newly single parent and the Senior Pastor at a church, the last thing I wanted to do was what I was doing. I know what Peter felt. For a portion of this particular transition I wanted to do nothing. I take that back, I wanted to run away. My nets were used and worn. I thought if I could get in a different place with different people, I could forget where I had been and what had happened. But I stayed in the manual and the scriptures began to come alive in me and healing my hurts by first healing my heart. I used the lessons that I was learning as the catalyst for what God was saying to our church. Throughout this entire transition I did not miss an opportunity to preach in church. Some of my dearest friends thought I should step down. To me that was like putting the nets away and saying I was done. I guess that voice of Jesus was whispering to me from the distance and telling me to stop putting the nets away because they were going to be needed. I did not want to stop in fact, I found that when things or people thought I should quit, I wanted to keep going even more! Like Peter, there was some reluctance but I was ready to move through this transition and do what the Lord was asking me to do. Though at times I thought that I had some better ideas. I truly believed that had I stopped, I would not be in a ministry occupation today. It was that important to keep my nets out. But that was a decision that I had to make.

Peter got back in his boat and took the other boat out as well to a deeper spot just as Jesus had said. It's okay to stop thinking shallow when the Lord says launch out. The same empty nets from the previous season were thrown off the sides of the boats and there it was...the most incredible surprise you could have imagined. Fish jumping into the nets, into the boats! So many fish that these nets were starting to break! So many fish that they had to signal for help to come and gather all of them into the boats! So many fish that they thought the boats might sink! Divine provision, God's abundant supply, prosperity, whatever you want to call it, Peter got blessed! All of them did! Can you get a picture in your mind for just a moment of you being happy again? Happier than you have ever thought was possible? Being in a spot where more and more people are working with you and believing in you?

Peter walked away from pride and found humility. Peter walked away from lack and found plenty. Peter walked away from his limitations and found God's abundance. Sometimes we have to leave a certain season that we had been in so that we can participate in a new season that God has prepared for us. As I counsel with many people who have endured a divorce, I see them trying to hold on to some of the things that they wanted. They stay attached to the same dependencies and never find the way to launch out deeper. They limit themselves by what they keep.

You cannot sail until you are willing to lose sight of the shore. Take the incredible life lessons of those other seasons and use them for your benefit. Peter took his gift, his boat and his nets and went back out on the lake. He took Jesus at His Word. Jesus took him to a spot he'd never dreamed of. A place he'd never been. Jesus gave him a new way to fish. And now that the nets were broken with the miraculous catch, Jesus would force him to get new nets! And suddenly, this tired, frustrated and discouraged man was surrounded by friends and partners gathering an incredible catch of fish. New energy was available. New help was all around. And a new day was born in the life of Peter...from now you will be a fisher of men.

Scripture says that for everything there is a season. A time for every purpose under heaven.(Ecclesiastes 3:1) I like seasons because the change often feels good. When the crisp air of fall comes in after the summer heat, I smile. When the white snow of winter arrives after the leaves fall, I laugh. When the snow melts with the spring sun and the flowers bloom again, I see once more the beauty of God coming alive right before my eyes. If you feel as though God has shut a door for you, the best thing you can do is to stop trying to go back and open it. While you may appear to be putting your nets away, God is setting things up for you to make another splash. He's preparing an incredible net-breaker for YOU! I know you may feel like you are going through all of this by yourself. You too may want to run away and never fish again. If you will hang in there and do what you know to do, God will prepare the way for you to do what only He can do. You have been programmed for success and no spouse, no employer, no drug or abusive situation can stop you from becoming all that He said you can be. My Bible tells me that I am the head and not the tail. I am above and not beneath. I am the righteousness of God in Christ Jesus and MY GOD shall supply ALL of my needs! I am free to be the me that He created me to be! Launch out! Let down your nets...not your hopes. And get ready to be pleasantly surprised!

Another TRANSITION story...

"Are you single or are you divorced? I actually thought I was single but the last time I went to the doctor's office I had to choose. Married, Single, or Divorced. I wrote in Single and Fabulous!

You are reading this book for a reason. I know you are because I have been in your same position. Moving from one season to the next takes a lot of guts and courage because most of the time, you don't get to pick the seasons. My season is married to divorced. I have a happy ending so I know that already you are hoping you can find similarities in my story that will match yours so that you know you're going to be ok. I know this because when my husband told me he wanted a divorce I read every book, listened to every self -help CD and T.V. show hoping that I would find the answer as if to say, "Tammy, this is what you do to get your husband back."

I will tell you now before you go any farther I didn't find my perfect solution. God is writing your story and it will be nothing like you had expected. So don't work too hard asking why.

I must have had people praying for me when I was pregnant and I knew deep down inside that something really bad was going to happen to me but I had this continuous thought in my head, "The footprints you see are not your own." I didn't have much peace and I was so scared but I could at least remember this thought.

It's a nervous feeling when you know someone else is occupying your spouse's time. It consumes your every waking moment. You struggle to function every day and you look to everyone except God to find the answer to your problem. You know your spouse is getting ready to walk and you hear them say things that don't make sense. "Stay strong for me."

When you hear them finally say they want out you will say a lot of emotional things because you just don't understand why they want to leave. And I hate to say it but you will probably act stupid, too, and regret a few dumb things you said or did. You know you would take them back. At that point in time you must take your eyes off the person that is hurting you because you can't change them and they will not be as remorseful as you want them to be. If they were they would come back. Trust me, if you took them back you would probably say things like, " I'll do anything you want." or "I promise I'll change." Listen to me. Don't even think about changing yourself. Think about asking for divine connections to guide you. Turn on Praise and Worship music. You'll cry a lot at first but that's ok. Hit your knees and tell God that you don't understand what is going on but tell him that you need him every second of the day from now on. Let him guide you. I took life 15 minutes at a time and still do.

During the divorce process, the custody battle and visitation rights will be hard but take your time and ask God to give you wisdom and boldness. Every mean word that someone says will hurt.

When the divorce is final, you will be relieved and excited and sad. You will be upset and cry that you are sleeping alone. Pray for emotional endurance. More importantly, pray that you have the strength to do things for others. Take the focus off you and enjoy your time alone if your children are with the other parent. Don't forget to pray for your child that angels will build a hedge around their bodies and their minds while they are away from you.

You will become beautiful again. You always were but this time it's different. You will begin to notice people smiling at you. You didn't notice before because you were too busy putting yourself down. Go on and admit that's what you were doing.

After all of this you just live every day to the fullest. You will learn to put a mental block against the lies that you hear. You might be ready to date or you might not. If you are bitter towards someone, it's because you don't have closure on that season and I hate to say it but they will not give you the closure you need. So, you close it for them. Your root of bitterness will vanish eventually. A new chapter begins but this time God is the author. And you are the star!!!"

"Tammy Duesler"

NOTE: Tammy Fuller transitioned back into her dream and became Mrs. Mark Duesler in my church on May 31 of 2008!

Chapter 9

Every week as I meet with the congregation of The Landing Community Church in Oklahoma, I see people from all walks of life. When we started this church in 2002, I was committed to go after people that had been wounded and bruised by the ministry or by ministers. I had no idea what I was going to see. Sitting right there in the midst of a wonderfully energized and anointed worship service were people that were contemplating suicide, young teens that were considering a departure from church life and seniors that believed their season for ministry was over. Often I would ask God to help me rise up out of that layer of hurt so that I could encourage people and truly give them a Word from the Lord. Each week my prayer would be "Lord, please send to our church today the people that you have handpicked to be impacted by the Word that you have laid upon my heart to share today." And each week they come. Many would "land" here as a final destination. Others would "layover" here. All will find a place where they could heal and be restored so that they could once again engage in society and evangelize those in their circle of influence. It's the last part of our mission statement. We call it E6. Our mission is: "to **enrich** and **encourage** people's lives by **equipping** and **empowering** them with the Word of God, so that they can **engage** in society and **evangelize** those in their circle of influence." It's what we do everyday at the Dreams2Destiny Center and each Sunday and Wednesday at The Landing Community Church.

Now you would think with a goal like that and a tremendous group of ministry-minded leaders, each and every person that lands here would be finely tuned and ready to fly again. In the middle of this anointed and contagious atmosphere, there is another type of person. They sit here week after week, month after month and year after year and nothing changes except their clothing. It reminds me of a man in the Bible in John 5.

> John 5:1 Some time later, Jesus went up to Jerusalem for a feast of the Jews. ²Now there is in Jerusalem near the Sheep Gate a pool, which in Aramaic is called Bethesda and which is surrounded by five covered colonnades. ³Here a great number of disabled people used to lie—the

blind, the lame, the paralyzed. ⁵One who was there had been an invalid for thirty-eight years. ⁶When Jesus saw him lying there and learned that he had been in this condition for a long time, he asked him, "Do you want to get well?"

⁷"Sir," the invalid replied, "I have no one to help me into the pool when the water is stirred. While I am trying to get in, someone else goes down ahead of me."

⁸Then Jesus said to him, "Get up! Pick up your mat and walk." ⁹At once the man was cured; he picked up his mat and walked.

The day on which this took place was a Sabbath, ¹⁰and so the Jews said to the man who had been healed, "It is the Sabbath; the law forbids you to carry your mat."

¹¹But he replied, "The man who made me well said to me, 'Pick up your mat and walk.' "

¹²So they asked him, "Who is this fellow who told you to pick it up and walk?"

¹³The man who was healed had no idea who it was, for Jesus had slipped away into the crowd that was there.

¹⁴Later Jesus found him at the temple and said to him, "See, you are well again. Stop sinning or something worse may happen to you." 15The man went away and told the Jews that it was Jesus who had made him well.

This man had been sick for 38 years. I can only imagine where his head was. Anytime that you are ill for that long, there is probably something inside of you that begins to accept the way things are. When you are in a transitional season you may find that something in you wants to sit down and say que sera, sera...whatever will be will be. I don't believe that this man had completely resolved that this was it because when Jesus showed up, he had energy...energy to make excuses. He blamed the people around him. He blamed timing. He blamed the environment that surrounded him. Jesus asked him what would appear to be a very simple question, "do you want to get well". The first time I read that part of the story, I think I laughed as if to say, what kind of question is that! Jesus, I have been immobile for 38 years and you are asking me if I want to get better? After thinking about that question for a while, I began to see that it was much deeper than I originally thought. When Jesus asks a question, it cuts to the bone. "Do you want to get well?". You see Jesus knew that a yes to that question would initiate a responsibility in a man that had done nothing for a long time. Saying yes means a life change. If you are healed, you will have to get some new clothes. If you are healed, you will have to get a job. If you are made well, you will have to find a new place to live. Have you considered what you will do when you get better?

I think that many people like being sick. They like having drama in their lives because the drama is what defines them. If there is no drama, they almost feel as though they have to create it so that they can have something to do. In your season of transition, you must consider what you will do WHEN you come through it. Notice I said WHEN. You see, as God begins your divine do-over or your new beginning, _you_ will have a responsibility to live your new life. That will mean old things are passed away. That means no more excuses as to why you are sick. When you have finished walking through this transition you will have to pick up your mat and move on. You take your mat with you because you never forget the lesson that you learned and where you came from.

You might be walking out of a very dark time. It may be painful. Still, God has used every terrible experience and painful attack to shape this person that He wants to utilize for His glory. You! He always has cared what has happened to you and that is why right now you are out of that other season and moving into this new one. You will have to answer this question about getting well with a resounding **yes**! You will have to leave this area surrounded by porches of difficulty. Let me take that a bit further.

In this story the Bible says that the pool where healing was available was surrounded by five porches. Imagine your new life in God, your dream, your fresh start being surrounded by porches that you will have to navigate around or step over to get to the place you need to be. There are always difficult things around the place that your were designed to be. I have defined these five levels as discouraged, diseased, delusional, disengaged and depression.

Level 1   **Discouraged**
"there was a great multitude of sick folks" God could never care about my troubles with all of these others! At this level there is a lack of courage because you feel that your situation is insignificant..

Level 2   **Diseased** Physical, emotional and mental
Internal illness that affects our thinking causing us to be fearful and to doubt that anything can change. We become "carriers" of diseased thinking

Level 3   <u>**Delusional**</u> reality is skewed by fantasy

Unable to see the supernatural for the natural. We get so caught up in what's going on that we cannot see what's happening.

Level 4   <u>**Disengaged**</u>

Un-attached, un-interested, un-willing to walk toward the "move" of God or the next season. Observer mentality. "I need to figure this out on my own"

Level 5   <u>**Depressed**</u>

Afraid it won't work, it won't last. Here we become depressed instead of impressed

To get well we will need to deal with these levels and conquer them. To conquer them will take support. To get support we have to stop making excuses.

We will always be around people that do not really want to get well. To get well means that they will have to change and some folks will never truly admit that they have a problem. Just let them sit there and sink. You are not a sinker! You have already decided that you need support and that you want to get well and that is why you are reading these words. You are an initiator. You make things happen and you are compelled to pursue destiny in every area of your life. You've said, YES! Lord, I want to get well! I want to move into the next season. I want to cross over to the other side. I know that I may enter some uncharted waters but I am ready for some net-breaking activity in my life. I'm ready for some new partners to help me gather in all of the blessings that are in store for me, my family and my future. It's time to pick up that mat, your life, and start moving forward again!

Chapter 10

I was always intrigued by the fact that Jesus told the man in our last story to take up his mat. I would think that if there was something that had been such an intricate part of my 38 year old illness that the moment I got off of it or out of it, I would say goodbye to it forever. Have you ever thought about that mat? Why would Jesus tell him to pick it up and take it with him? That's the way I read that story, the man took it with him.

Perhaps the mat was to serve as a reminder of what Jesus had just done. Maybe it would be used as part of an illustrated testimony as he shared the story about his healing with others. Or it could be that many of the things we transition out of seem to stay with us through the rest of our lives in the lessons that were learned and the struggles that were endured. There is not one day that goes by that I don't feel sad about going through the season of divorce. It has been several years now and I am still transitioning. My mat is with me everyday in the form of my children that I see and love and continue to nurture. My mat is right beside me every night as I sleep in my bed alone. The fact of the matter is the mat goes with me because that season will always be a part of my life. I've gone through the terrible counseling sessions where people tell me to "get over it" and people say "the pain and hurt will go away". **I believe that you don't get over some things, you endure them.** The difference is that they do not change the course of your future but they have brought you to your present. The lesson had to be learned and there is part of your character that had to be shaped. Accepting your part in this process is very therapeutic.

How do you tell someone who has lost a child to get over it? Periodically they look at the little clothes and walk through their room. Things like this sting. Still, it is the stinging that lets us know there is still life in us. If it no longer hurt, we'd no longer be living. We've got to feel these things because they are the very feelings that will guide us through this transitional time.

When Jesus told this man to rise and take up his mat, the thing I want you to notice is that for the very first time in 38 years, <u>the mat did not hold</u>

<u>him, he held the mat</u>. The mat was no longer a platform for misery; it was a tool for ministry. It's in that moment that you and I begin to realize that the transitional season is coming to an end and we are about to walk into the new season. The history is still there. The pain still comes and goes. But now your test blossoms into a test-imony.

As I have leaned upon my personal character building lessons and offered counsel to others that had not yet divorced but were on their way towards it, I have noticed that my strength to endure gets stronger each time. It's as if each day the Lord is saying, "you said you wanted to get well" and this is part of being made whole. We are made whole by taking our mat and helping others see that they matter.

Many of you will read this chapter and say to yourself that you are not ready to share your story at this time. Let me assure you that this is normal and perfectly fine. You see, you are in a transition and only you and your God can work through the things that you are learning and the character that is building in you. I am certain that there will come a moment when you rise, take up your mat and walk. I am certain that every person you minister to by using your mat will make you a little bit stronger. And as you gain more and more strength you find your way into the next season that was being prepared for you while you were being prepared for it.

One thing that I have experienced and learned so far (I say so far because I learn something everyday), God knows what He is doing and His timing is perfect. I have realized that He is never early and that He is never late. I have come to the place many times where I feel like I am beaten again and lying on my back on that dirty old mat. Yes, there are times when I still feel hopeless and my heart still hurts. But before it gets the best of me, I feel His loving arms embrace me. Often, no words are shared and no outward changes take place. Still I know that I am being transformed into someone that makes Him happy. I am being renewed and refreshed from the inside out. And then I notice, right there on the couch, my mat. Perhaps it's time to use it again to help someone else. And I go.

Chapter 11

Every time that I type the words directly above this sentence, Chapter 11, I am reminded of the other part of my divorce transition. Bankruptcy. Going from having money to having NO money. A rupture of your personal bank account. Bankruptcy. That word used to be much more powerful and harmful than it seems to be today. In fact when companies cannot make ends meet, they file bankruptcy and change the name to try again. Often the only thing that really changes is the name. My financial transition occurred in my life at the same time the personal one did.

I was raised to understand that if you worked hard and made good decisions, saved your money and loved God, your life would be fruitful. I still believe that. What hindered me in this transition is that I made some decisions that were not so good and that is why I was in a mess. I had saved some money in the past but I had used it to begin the ministry of Dreams2Destiny Center and my personal dream of The Landing Community Church. So the divorce was in motion, my finances were completely out of whack and I was running in circles. I went to a handful of debt consolidators over a 2 month period. I had done this before. There was no possible way to make the payments that they were advising me to make and live a normal life. I am sure that some of you have been there before. Because my heart was completely crushed and my spirit waning, I had no fight in me for this financial piece of the puzzle. I gave in to the bankruptcy and let all of the stuff go. There are times today that I wonder what may have happened if I did not give in. I walked into this transition completely aware of what it would mean to my financial life but not completely aware of what it might do to my personal life. My credit score was the least of my troubles.

To be honest, the loss of someone that I cared so deeply for was so devastating to me that the bankruptcy meant nothing at the time. All of this was becoming one horrific wake-up call. It was like being in a deep sleep and thinking you set your alarm for a soft buzz in the morning only to be awakened by heavy metal music at the highest possible volume level! I used this awakening as a catalyst to tell myself that my finances would never be in that position again. I would live on cash and everything would be fine. What I found out was how hard it would be to follow through. I was starting all over again. I transitioned from a house to an apartment. I had to get one with a few bedrooms because I had three kids that would spend some time with me each week. I began to see that by the time all of the expenses were paid and the needs were met, living on cash meant having no money left over. At first this was very difficult. It was hard because I was still carrying the memories of what used to be and what I used to have. I even found myself at times driving in my old neighborhood to look at my previous house. Sounds silly doesn't it? Each time it hurt. But then something clicked inside. It was like a light switch just came on. I had been somewhat successful in my work and had acquired many things. But I realized that <u>I did not have these things, they had me</u>.

It was at that point that I wrote a **goodbye letter.** I started to write down a list of all of the things that I wanted to say goodbye to. I wrote them out on a legal pad. I said goodbye to all of the things that had trapped me. All of the stuff that I thought I had to acquire. All of those attitudes that kept me in financial bondage. I said goodbye to a life of credit card debt and bills that could never be paid. I wrote down relationship things, emotional things and spiritual things. All this was in my goodbye letter and then I stuffed it away in a drawer.

After the goodbyes had been said, it was time to say hello to a new normal. That's right, I had to look at my life with this new normal. It was not something I was used to. It was foreign territory. I said hello to having enough cash to pay the bills. I said hello to being the greatest dad I could be and thinking of new ways to have fun with my children without spending money. I never knew that was possible! I said hello to responsibility for my actions and seeking out the things and the people that gave me life and hope and health. I said hello to the promise that no weapon formed against me can prosper and I began to profess what God had already said about me...I am the head and not the tail and I am above and not beneath. I have not failed. I am still going! Day by day, little by little, the clarity was coming. I was honoring the Lord by paying my tithes and even helping the church get some things that they needed. I would take people to lunch and bless them knowing that every seed I planted was going to produce a harvest. "I" was showing up in my life again, only I was different. I was beginning to see who I really was and what made me tick. It was a new normal and each day I am being made new to deal with this new normal.

Understand that my circumstances are no different. I could not borrow money right now if I wanted to. Still today, because I am looking at things with different glasses, God has truly blessed me. I have a gorgeous home that I lease instead of an apartment. I'm no longer leasing a car, I own one! And I have all that I need to live my new normal life. Scripture says, "My God shall supply all of my need according to His riches in glory". I am living with that promise moment by moment and day by day. God is always faithful.

I think that because there were two terrible things happening in my life simultaneously, it allowed me to mix them together and not go through double denial and anger and bargaining etc. I really did have to endure the transition of divorce and bankruptcy. And today I see so many horrible tragedies in life that are so much worse than either of those. Your personal situation and the transition that you are in right now may be one of those. Perception of what is going on and prayer can become two keys to help you endure. Maybe you need to write your own goodbye letter. Someone once told me "on the paper, off the mind". If you know the Lord, you can be certain that your situation is being mixed and mingled with grace and mercy and that you will rise up through this transition in a better place than you have ever been. God will create a new normal for you. As you notice these subtle yet distinct changes, acknowledge the very fact that you can see God showing up for you in the midst of your crossing over experience. For every thing that comes against you God promises to bring something more for you. Say hello to those new things and know that you are valuable to Him and you matter deeply. You are the head and not the tail. You are above and not beneath. You are MORE than a conqueror through Jesus Christ! Say it with me…."New normal, here I come!"

Chapter 12

At some point in the journey into the next season of life through the transitional season you need friends. What has interested me in putting this book together is the variety of ways that people deal with that time in the middle...between where you were and where you are going. I have shared some of those stories with you. We all deal with those "life happens" moments differently. Yet I have noticed something that was consistent in each person I have talked to regarding transitions. They all were looking for someone to talk to, connect with, get support from. Some of them did it consciously and some subconsciously. We were created to be with other people and to learn and lean upon each other. I noticed in my conscious pursuit of fellowship and counsel that there is a support group for everything and everyone... almost. I needed a friend. I didn't need 12 steps, I wanted one giant leap to my final destination: the new me with my new normal. I discovered a variety of groups to go to if I was a woman and my husband had left me. They were all meeting on Wednesday nights and since I had a church of my own and services on Wednesday, that would never be possible. I found no group for men that have been in my situation. I wondered is I was the only guy to ever go through this. I felt so isolated yet I was starved for an environment filled with people. You would think that having a couple of hundred folks to minister to every Sunday morning would satisfy but it does not even scratch the spot that is itching. God created me and you for connectedness...to be attached to people with similar interests and circumstances. We seem to gravitate towards those people naturally but when life takes a negative turn on you the natural is blown out and we must readjust to what happened.

What made it more difficult for me was the fact that my old normal kept trying to show up again. My old normal was to shut off and not even think or talk about things again. I guess that is the denial. Yet, each time that a person in our church wanted to seek spiritual counsel I found myself living my story over and over again. What was interesting to me was the spiritual insight that I had gained from walking in the midst of my personal circumstances.

I was able to provide some godly counsel to others and the words that came out of my mouth seemed to be fashioned by the very hand of God. Couples would stay together, begin working on plans to make their marriage better. I started to see that their support was not coming from me, it was coming from the Lord. As long as they trusted God and took Him at His Word they were moving forward. But the minute their eyes came off of Christ, the trouble showed up again and this time it brought friends!

I encourage the people of our church to think about their Five...that is, to decide who is in their Five. You know, just like the cell phone carrier. Everyone needs a few folks to bounce things off of and share their victories and challenges with. People they can trust and become a team with. I began to be a part of a group of men like that and we started brainstorming, ideating,(like IBM) and looking forward to what God had planned for us. We knew that there was a collection of "dreams" within us that God had in mind for us to do when he created us but like most people, we got busy and the busyness became our business. As we became account-able to each other God lit a flame. It started as a spark and began to grow. Our dreams became plans and we started writing these things down and supporting them with the scriptures that the Lord was showing us. Let me tell you what is so great about it for me. We don't spend a lot of time talking about what is wrong. We use the time to develop things that are right. And God seems to be pleased with that. Things we have prayed about and asked for God to show up in are coming to fruition and we are acknowledging that every good and perfect gift is indeed from Him.

Now that fire is beginning to burn through some other folks and they are putting together their groups to share and grow in grace. The hardest part of finding your own five is getting it started. Think about your hand for a moment. Look at it. Counting your thumb you have five moving parts. They can form a fist or they can work together or individually. They can help lift things, hold a pencil or make a peace sign! Imagine you are number one, the index finger and each of the other fingers and the thumb represent a person that you are connected to. A person that you like being around and that you would consider a friend. Invite your fingers over to the house for some coffee and a dessert and see what happens. Just start talking. Share your own personal insights and lessons that

YOU are learning as you LIVE your life. Then add the blueprint for life, the Word of God to the discussion and watch the insight and answers that you are given from your Heavenly Father who loves you. **You** will <u>receive</u> counsel and you will <u>give</u> it. You will be amazed at some of the things that come out of your mouth! You will be speaking out of the abundance of your heart and God will use your group to work things out and bring others into the right place in their lives. I said earlier that there was no support group for what I had been through...the male perspective. God showed me that I did not need a group that talked about where I was. He wanted me to be part of one that would see where I was going!

Who is in your Five? Get your hand together and see what God can do in you and through you!

Lord, who can I begin to "dream" with and become a blessing to? Show me the five people that would be blessed by you and that could be beneficial to me and my healing process in the transitional seasons that I am going through. Help me to be a blessing to each of them as well and help each of us work together so that we can all move towards what you have designed us for.

Now take a moment and write down the names of YOUR Five:

1 ME

2 _____

3 _____

4 _____

5 _____

Ask the Lord to give you favor and an opportunity to begin gathering them together.

Chapter 13

How are you doing so far? Are you still with me? Did the Lord help put your hand together? You will need that hand at some point in your future so keep trying to put it in place. You may find that it is too hard to get 4 others right now and if that is your situation, I would suggest that you start with what you have. It may be one or two to begin with. Just begin the process and see what God wants to do.

One of the most pronounced things that I see and hear every day is that my life is different. Not bad, different. A couple of chapters ago I used the phrase "new normal". I cannot truly say that there is an appearance of anything normal at this point. I am still in transition as I am writing this book! Remember I said that you do not get over it, you endure it.

One important thing to do when you are crossing over to the other side is to keep your eyes on your destination. I have talked to many people who often focus on their desperation and then wind up missing their destination. They get so caught up in the transition season that they miss the object of the transition. It is possible to be so consumed by what is happening around you that you don't see what is happening to you. God often makes subtle changes that may or may not be noticed on a daily basis. Perhaps you have experienced that already. You woke up one day to realize that you were so much farther down the road to recovery than you thought and you can't remember any major thing that happened to get you there. It's because little by little, adjustments have been made on the journey you are taking to the other side. As you go through the transition, God is on your side and helping you to steer clear of what can harm you and gravitate towards what can heal you.

Remember earlier when we discussed the story about crossing over to the other side which we found in Mark 4? If you finish reading the story you can see that it says "when they reached the other side!" Thank God we do get to the other side! But don't start your touchdown celebration just yet. What happens when the place that you get to isn't really what you thought it would be when you started there?

Jesus had told His disciples to go and they left. The storm had rose up and they all thought they were dead and then just as quickly as it came…Jesus spoke and it left. They came to the place that I assume they were going since Jesus is in control. The land is called Gerasenes. And what happens next you just have to read…

> Mark 5:2 When Jesus got out of the boat, a man with an evil spirit came from the tombs to meet him. [3]This man lived in the tombs, and no one could bind him any more, not even with a chain. [4]For he had often been chained hand and foot, but he tore the chains apart and broke the irons on his feet. No one was strong enough to subdue him. [5]Night and day among the tombs and in the hills he would cry out and cut himself with stones.

As soon as they arrived at the place that they were going, their destination, a man with an evil spirit came out of the tombs to meet them. Not the Welcome Wagon they were hoping for! The Bible says that this man could no longer be restrained. He actually tore through the chains and broke the irons that held his feet. He was possessed and no one was strong enough to subdue him. At night he would cry out loud and cut himself with stones.

Now this is not the picture that I was hoping to see when we crossed over to the other side. I was looking for something a bit more peaceful and reserved...a place where healing lived rather than where healing was needed. Then it dawned on me...I went through a transition to help someone else go through theirs!

I have to tell you that I talk to more divorced people today than I ever have in the past. Why? Because God knows that I can relate to what they are feeling and going through. He knows that I will dispense His Word to them and pray that they can follow His plan through. Each day I may get another opportunity to use a lesson that I have learned to help someone else pass their test. That makes me feel a sense of purpose and value that was nearly stripped from me at the beginning of this journey. My perception of things has changed.

I know that there are many people out there that are being controlled by things that have them bound in chains. They even act like they are out of their mind. What may look like a surprise ambush is really a predetermined opportunity to continue your healing. You see when you can take your eyes off of your situation and help someone else in theirs; you shift momentum in YOUR favor. The interesting part of this encounter to me is that it happened immediately when they got to the other side. There was no time to prepare or make allowances for what might happen. Immediately a man from the tombs came toward Jesus. It's as if he wants us to realize that the journey over the lake has already done some work in us and we are ready for whatever may come upon us. What we may have perceived as a terrible lake disaster was really a character growth seminar and more wisdom and power had been planted in us during the entire ordeal. Imagine that! A storm that makes you a better person! All the time you were learning! And you thought you were fighting to save your life!

Don't be surprised when the very thing that came against you comes back at you in another form as you reach the "other side" of your transition. You are blessed to be a blessing and that will mean that your experience will teach others how to make it through what you are going through. Initially I was not prepared to encounter couples that were facing what I had faced. I was a bit ambushed by how quickly they came as I was trying to climb out of my hole and back into society again. I was not fearful...I was faithful. I simply took each meeting and encounter as another chance to use the tools that I had been given and put into play the lessons that I had learned. And you know what happened? People were helped! As I was ministering I was continuing to learn and it was amazing!

Now I want you to notice in this story that this man who was uncontrollable and "had issues" was always under the power of Christ. What was controlling him was still subject to the authority of Jesus and that is why the spirits controlling him bowed before Christ and began the dialogue. They knew the end result of a Jesus encounter...demons gone, angels victorious! I chuckle when I think about how they begged not to be tormented. The chief of all tormentors asking not to be tormented! Jesus did not negotiate or try to be rational with these irrational spirits...he just called them out.

The longer you try to negotiate the more you may end up surrendering. You and I do not have to have a discussion with the things that keep coming after us, we simply tell them to go. I remember when I was first trying to forget all of the stuff that happened at the end of my marriage, I would treat my mind like a computer and every time I had a thought or saw an image I did not like, I would say out loud DELETE! No matter where I was or what I was doing I was attempting to take captive these thoughts and subject them to what God had to say. In the store or in the car, you would hear every once in a while, DELETE, DELETE. What was happening was that I was conditioning myself to no longer engage in conversations and ideas that were not healthy. If it did not breath life and joy into me than I rejected it. And every time I said delete I imagined that the thought or image was being erased from my hard drive.

I like the story in Mark because the demons that were controlling this poor soul knew they were destined to die and the first thing they say they wanted to enter...PIGS! Send us into the pigs, they cried. Notice that they needed permission from Jesus to go anywhere. Jesus sent the demonic spirits into the pigs and the pigs started acting like the man...uncontrollable and out of their little pig minds! The Bible says that there were 2000 pigs in that gathering and they ran off a cliff and drowned in the sea.

Another soul had been rescued for eternity. There was probably a lesson coming for whoever owned those pigs too! YOU have a purpose and a value to the Lord. What happens TO you can make great changes in what happens IN you. Just because you get to the other side of this transitional season does not mean that all of the struggles and tough encounters will cease. They may just take on a different form but you will have more and more strength each time to deal with them.

Now I know that since you are reading this book, you may be a lot like me and you can name the pigs that you would like to send those demons into! You'd like a front row seat on the edge of the cliff so you could watch those crazy pigs jump! Feelings of wanting to feel vindicated and justified will always be a part of your nature. Just remember that God is the judge and He has the control over what happens to you. And I can assure you, He will take care of the pigs!

More Transitions Stories...

One of the most recent transitions in my life began in July of 2007. I have been a hairdresser for 18 years. In July God started leading me to do something different. We had an after school program at church and I had no desire to be a part of it but God had a different plan for me. I had a full time job how could I have another job? God took my full time job and turned it into a part time one. I followed where God was leading me although it wasn't my desire and was completely out of my comfort zone. In Sept.2007 I starting running the after school program., a month later the boss of the center encouraged me to go to school to get my CDA, it was a struggle but I made A's so I felt like this was part of Gods plan for me. After a few weeks I realized this was where I was supposed to be and loved my job .Everything went great for a couple of months then the bottom fell out of the learning center. The next few months was the most stressful time in my life .Things were happening that I didn't agree with and co-workers were doing things that I didn't feel was right. On Feb.16th 2008 I was fired from my job. Boy! that was a blow to my ego! Although it was a relief, I was emotionally exhausted. I spent days questioning God "why did you bring me here to get fired!" I felt all this hard work was for nothing. Well, I just took one day at a time and totally trusted God to carry me through. I also prayed a lot more in every situation I faced, read my Bible daily. Also I got a lot of WISE council *from my pastors and their teachings (sermons) kept me encouraged. They told me that this is just a season and to keep believing and have faith that God is in control of every situation.*

It was totally God in the whole thing. He really matured me and I grew spiritually, I truly believe I didn't have that personal relationship with Him that was necessary and now I can honestly say I rely on Him for everything.

Pam Culbertson

Chapter 14

Lakes, nets, storms, pigs...you may be thinking, who is this guy that is writing this book? Don't analyze it too hard. I'm just trying to live a life that pleases God and brings Him glory! Just as I think out loud often, I guess I write books the same way! Remember, we are all going through some sort of transition. I cannot reiterate enough that it is more important what is happening IN you than what is happening TO you. Something great will rise up and show itself as you press on. The Bible talks about forgetting what is behind and straining towards what is ahead. It's so important to keep something out in front of us to walk towards. Lack of vision causes people to give up. When we lose the will to keep moving it will not be long before we stop alto-gether. I have had many people in my life that care about me, that encourage me with words, and that feels wonderful. But unless I can see something in my heart of hearts, unless God allows me to continue dreaming and being creative, I am certain I would fizzle out. I run this race of life in a way like I am going to win and there is a huge trophy waiting for me WHEN I finish, not IF I finish. I have a goal and that goal is what God says I can be and who God says I am. Sometimes that is the only thing that gets me up in the morning.

One of the most important lessons that I am learning through the transitions in my life is how important it is to take care of me. That used to sound so selfish to me. I would feel guilty anytime that I did anything for myself and if I were honest I would tell you that I probably condemned myself. I matter to God! Remember the "I" right there in the middle of that word transitions! Taking care of me seemed to go against the grain of looking out for the best of others and honoring their needs. What made things worse is that I was a pastor and people relied on me. I would find myself in situations where others had no idea what was happening in my life and what I was going through so for them it was business as usual. I began to see that if I did not force myself to take breaks and recharge myself, I could not help anyone. Yes, it was true that God wanted to use my experiences to help others. But the fact of the matter for me was that there were days when I knew that I should not do anything because I felt emotionally weak and mentally exhausted. I remembered how the Lord at times would attempt to go into the mountains to pray and get away. Sometimes he would succeed and other times the need would follow him. In my life I was amazed at how God would speak words through me when they were necessary even if I did not have personal strength. I totally understood what He meant when He said that in my weakness He would be made strong. When Jesus told us to love our neighbors as ourselves, he was saying something similar to what I am sharing with you. He was telling us that you and I need to learn to love ourselves. I mean to be happy with the person that God created in His image. He created us just the way we are and we need to be pleased with that and have a good self-image and see ourselves as He sees us. It is only then that we will be able to effectively love others. Maybe the problem with many of our relationships is that we really do love others as we love ourselves and the truth is that <u>we do not love ourselves</u>!

As I mentioned in a previous chapter, I was trying to discover me and what I liked to do. I tried to write down a list of things that I <u>loved</u>, things that I <u>liked</u> and things that I <u>did not like</u>. That was an interesting exercise. If you have never done that you may surprise yourself by trying it! When you really begin to look inward at what ignites your spirit and what truly touches your heart you begin to see the amazing person that God created you to be. You get a glimpse of the possibilities you have if you can solidify the relationship you have with your Creator. And you start to understand what He meant when he said He would give you **rest** when you were weary and weighted down by life's burdens. I began to understand that when the Lord speaks of rest, he is not talking to us about inactivity. It is more about an exchange of our burdens for his. Lighter loads use less energy and therefore are more restful than heavier ones. You may not have to stop what you are doing if you are able to cast your cares upon Him.

I must warn you about how challenging it will be to create personal time for YOU to recharge and refresh. I have found in my routine that I must schedule rest time or book writing and song writing time just as any other meeting. If I do not plan in advance to take those moments I will jump into something else and before long I have worn myself out and mentally I am completely drained. Each of us needs a rest and recharge season. How you recharge is also important. It does not mean that you always have to be alone and in a quiet place. One of the ways you can replenish yourself is when you gather each week with your local body of believers for fellowship. God created us for community...to connect with one another and to share life experiences with each other. Being in an energized group of people that are going to the same place and have the same drive will be exhilarating. When the church began with a small group of people, God was putting an atmosphere of hope and encouragement together that would last forever. The church IS the people...organic...evolving and full of vibrant life. It was to be like "flowing" water and never stagnant. When you and I can exchange our burdens for what the Lord would have us carry, it will feel like rest compared to always having to work things out for ourselves. Every person that I have talked to about their transitional seasons has found their own personal way to deal with their mind, body and spirit. Some of their thoughts I have passed on in the stories shared in this book. You will write one too. And what works for you is what is important.

Take a few moments today to consider how well you are maintaining yourself. Your body is called the temple of the Holy Spirit...you are a container and you cannot afford to become cracked or broken. The world cannot afford to lose the gift that God gave to you! If you realize that things have gotten away from you and you have no time for yourself, I encourage you today to begin placing YOU on your schedule. Maybe you start with a walk through the neighborhood or a drive in the country. Perhaps you relax at the local coffee shop with your journal and write down your thoughts. Right now, it's about YOU and YOU being the person that you were meant to be. No one can steal that from you. Nothing that has happened to you can rob you of the glorious future that you were designed to live. Your BEST can be the REST of your life!

"Nothing can separate you from the love of God"

Romans 8:38,39

Chapter 15

I am learning more things about me as I am writing this book! I just realized something today. While I am writing about these transitional seasons, several of them are happening around me and in me right now! As I am writing down thoughts from my heart to help you move forward, God has been moving things forward for our ministry! I have been thinking and writing forward (maybe its like paying it forward) and the Lord has been guiding me to the other side in so many ministry areas. I was not even thinking about our ministry and what we are doing because I have been mentally and emotionally tied to this book. God is taking care of me as I do what He inspires me to do! And I believe that the same thing will happen for you too!

That is a principal that I think we often overlook in transitions. In most of my personal trips to the other side I have been consumed by me and what I need and by what I have to have. I would worry about whether I would make it to the other side? I wondered if I would I like it and would it be what I want? The more I analyzed it the less I moved in a forward direction. I would actually lose any momentum that I had gained because these types of feelings and emotions bogged me down. You've probably heard the phrase "one step forward and two steps back". That is exactly how it felt for me. I can't really say that I remember when I said to myself that I was sick and tired of being sick and tired. I am not sure that there was a single highlight or defining moment when lights and bells went off. It was almost like the Lord was changing things about me little by little and they were so subtle that when I had actually transformed it seemed like it happened right away! I began to get healthy! As I started to get healthy in my mind, will and emotions and as I took care of myself, my natural instincts to serve others and help them began to be engaged again. You have heard people talk about things that they do by saying that " it just comes naturally". What you are supernaturally created to do appears to come naturally when you are in your right mind and healthy. When you feel good you express good things. When you are weak, tired, nearing burn-out, not much good emits off of you. You see when I was overwhelmed by my past and what happened to me I was hindered from being the over-comer that Christ made me to be. To be an over-comer means that you come-over to the other side. It means you get through the transition and to the destination.

Realize this...when you move in the direction of what you were created to do, you cannot fail. There may be challenges and even a few obstacles but **you were created for this!** You are wired to succeed! I remember looking at a picture on the church wall of the vision and dream that I felt that the Lord had given to me. The problem for me was that I associated that image with my marriage and because my marriage was over I pictured God's dream that He had shared to both of us as being obsolete. I can still remember the day that I took this image off of the wall, took it out of the frame and rolled it up. I stopped talking about where we were going as a faith community. For a season I really did not have a goal...I was just floating. Imagine that...the man that penned the book turning your Dreams2Destiny stopped talking about the destination! If you read my last book, you already know what happened after that! Remember that song...gloom, despair and agony on me! It was deep dark depression, excessive misery. If it weren't for bad luck I'd have no luck at all! All of a sudden I was in a maintenance mode and this was a job. I quit watching God fulfill His dream in me. I was so busy operating in survival mode that I lost sight of the very things that compelled me to move to the other side in the first place. And then I heard something within the deepest part of my being. I'd like to say that I heard the audible voice of God but that just did not happen. I felt a prompting on the inside. As I gave way to this inner-leading, it was telling me that the dream that God breathed...that image on the paper was something He desired. It did not matter whether I was married, or single, or rich or poor. He had offered me the opportunity to move it forward. His plan and purpose would prevail. He would do it with or without me and that would be the choice I must make.

I went back to the office with a smile in my heart and on my face and I got that picture back out, put it in a frame and placed it upon the wall. I told the Lord that this image was the other side of a very difficult transition for me and I was not going to stop until He said stop. I accepted what was going on inside of me as His purpose. Let me tell you what that did for me.

Each day that I would come to the church, I saw where God was taking me. People that visited our church saw where God was taking us. It energized me and put a target out in front of me once more. I had been ignited once again. And that was only the beginning. I decided to change the name of our facility that we were renting as a church and it became the Dreams2Destiny Center. Not only would it house the church but also a community driven food and clothing pantry called The Glenpool Outreach Center. I saw children being educated in the arts and an idea for an after school program that was all about drama, music and the arts was born called Xpressions. Suddenly, there was a buzz in the air...something to talk about...something to see. God started to direct people to the church and the energy level of our entire church increased! It probably felt the same way the disciples felt when Jesus got into that boat after calming the storm and teaching Peter about how to "walk on the water". When Jesus is there, all is well!

What I have discerned through this particular season and transition is that I must have a picture of where I am going in front of me. Sometimes it is tangible and sometimes I have to IMAGEine it. I have to create an image to look at in my mind.

When I play golf I visualize my shot hitting the green. In baseball I see the bat hit the ball. In counseling couples that are struggling, I see them completely restored and doing great things for God. And for the church we call The Landing, I see people that are sick being made complete and whole again. I see innovative ideas being birthed and new songs written. I see ordinary people doing extraordinary things and making the world realize that with God ALL things are truly possible!

Perhaps you need some images out in front of you. Transitions are not known for their clarity and you may have to ask God to give you some glimpse of what lies ahead. The great part is that He will give you whatever you need whenever you need it. Like that picture on my wall of the Dreams2Destiny Center Campus, your images will energize you and put a smile on your face and in your heart. And that just makes everything come together a little bit easier!

Before you finish this chapter and begin the next, set this book down and begin to imagine yourself in the place that your heart is telling you to be. See yourself in that environment and surrounded by those people. Get a very clear and vivid picture in your mind and ask God to keep it in front of all those trying situations and negative feelings. When we begin to see the things that He desires for us to see, we will see our passion rekindled and our enthusiasm about moving through this transition increase. What do you see? Is it in color? Are you smiling yet?

Write down what you were looking at.

_____

_____

_____

_____

_____

_____

_____

Chapter 16

I am somewhat of a competitor in just about everything I do. Like many people, I do not like to lose in any type of contest and I don't like to feel like I am behind. We have identified the fact that all of us are going through some sort of a transition in life and dealing with it however we can. It's a process and hopefully we are becoming sensitive to ourselves through this process. Remember that story about Peter standing up and jumping out of the boat to walk on the water? Have you ever thought about what the other disciples in the boat were thinking? I wonder if anyone was envious? Jealous? Angry? I wonder if any of the other guys actually prayed that he would not succeed.

I know that sounds ridiculous but unfortunately in ministry today and in the church world those feelings run rampant. As small groups transition today into actual church fellowships they can begin to notice that not everyone in the community will be excited that they are there to help. Not everyone is going to jump on board with God's dream for you. Just remember that He gave it to YOU and not them! Often even in church transitions we start to look at how our transition is going compared to another church's. That can get discouraging. Too often, all we care about are the numbers of people coming when the Lord is really after the number of lives changed. I asked someone working at another church the other day how they were doing and they said great...and then they told me their weekly attendance!

God did not call us to **compete** with people. He called us to **complete** people. Each gathering of faithful followers has a unique way to do this and we must always make sure we stay focused on what we are to do and not comparing it to what someone else is doing.

It shows up in personal struggles too. When my ex-wife got remarried I hit the bottom of that barrel again. I was sad about what happened and honestly I felt sorry for myself all over again. I felt like she succeeded and I was failing because I was not even close to where she was. God, why has she moved on and I am still in the same place? But I wasn't in the same place, I had moved on too. I had just been guided on a different highway. The good news is that I did not live at the bottom of this barrel as long as I did when divorce first shocked me. I did not check into the self-pity hotel for an extended stay. Instead I was able to rid my competing spirit by acknowledging this completing spirit. I began to see this event for me as a completion of a transitional season. Interestingly enough it brought a level of closure for me and the shoreline of the other side was now in visible sight. I wondered if that theory of completing versus competing would work for other things. I remembered a scripture I had read before..."pray one for another that YOU may be healed." In other words, the Bible tells me that if I will focus on meeting another person's need, mine will be met on the way! Again it sounds like a pay it forward approach doesn't it?

So, maybe one way to move through a transition season is to help someone else move through theirs! I have to admit that this was quite a revelation for me. I've heard motivational speakers and leadership experts talk about how success comes from learning how to solve other people's problems. I think they were talking in terms of the fact that people will pay you for answers. God pays you with huge benefits when you look out for the needs of those around you over your own. It does not mean that you think less of yourself...you just think of yourself less!

If we are all going through some type of transition, why not look closely at those around you to see who you can assist. What if people started to look at you to complete them rather than compete with them? A turnaround is waiting and all you have to do is take that first step.

Chapter 17

By now you have probably experienced a variety of emotions in reading through these pages. You may even be riding a rollercoaster of feelings and thoughts. I think that is the struggle and the beauty of transitions. Taking those first steps may look like watching a toddler learn the art of walking. It looks awkward and sometimes funny. But if you keep watching, one day very soon there will be a fluid motion of steps and you will grow weary just trying to keep up with them!

For me I must always remind myself that I am learning and growing even when it feels like I am being beaten and destroyed. I must always remember that Christ is leading my life and that where I go and who I run into is all being orchestrated as I flow in His will for my life. Jesus always sends us into places that we can do the greatest good. But it doesn't always mean that everyone will be happy we are there. Look at this story...

[1]He called his twelve disciples to him and gave them authority to drive out evil[a] spirits and to heal every disease and sickness.

[2]These are the names of the twelve apostles: first, Simon (who is called Peter) and his brother Andrew; James son of Zebedee, and his brother John; [3]Philip and Bartholomew; Thomas and Matthew the tax collector; James son of Alphaeus, and Thaddaeus; [4]Simon the Zealot and Judas Iscariot, who betrayed him.

[5]These twelve Jesus sent out with the following instructions: "Do not go among the Gentiles or enter any town of the Samaritans. [6]Go rather to the lost sheep of Israel. [7]As you go, preach this message: 'The kingdom of heaven is near.' [8]Heal the sick, raise the dead, cleanse those who have leprosy,[b]drive out demons. Freely you have received, freely give. [9]Do not take along any gold or silver or copper in your belts; [10]take no bag for the journey, or extra tunic, or sandals or a staff; for the worker is worth his keep.

[11]"Whatever town or village you enter, search for some worthy person there and stay at his house until you leave. [12]As you enter the home, give it your greeting. [13]If the home is deserving, let your peace rest on it; if it is not, let your peace return to you. [14]If anyone will not welcome you or listen to your words, shake the dust off your feet when you leave that home or town. [15]I tell you the truth, it will be more bearable for Sodom and Gomorrah on the day of judgment than for that

town. [16]I am sending you out like sheep among wolves. Therefore be as shrewd as snakes and as innocent as doves.

Jesus called the guys together and sent them out. Notice that He did not send them out ill equipped...He gave them authority and they had within them the power to transform lives just as He had done. In fact scripture says that every sickness and disease was subject to their power. In verses 7-10 He gets a bit more specific and reminds them not to worry about anything but the task. In other words do not allow yourself to get bogged down in the details. That means don't keep rehashing what is right and wrong in your mind and keeping yourself from being focused on where God is sending you. He is trying to teach them how to "live" faith. He wants them to learn how to go to a place that He has sent them and be provided for as they need support. It is a pilgrimage of sorts as they go from city to city without many of life's luxuries, just that anointing service and command from Jesus to go.

Let me interject something here. Don't forget who sent you and what they did to prepare you for being sent. You probably feel like you are in this transition because you lost something or someone or it/they have been taken away. Try to reframe your thought process to see yourself being guided in a different direction and being led by the most incredible power on the planet to the place that that power can be fully utilized in your life. Sitting alone and isolating yourself while replaying ideas that you have been robbed or that life and joy have been stolen is not what can bring you through. Can I share part of my heart with you here?

When my life changed and all of a sudden, my life partner was not there, I spent a great deal of time yelling at the devil. I cried repeatedly because I had just lost my buddy and my friend. I had been stripped of the mother of our children and I was emotionally overwhelmed. One day as I was having another why God? party something inside my heart released that way of thinking. I stopped yelling at the devil and started to listen to God. And what I heard sounded weird at first but each day I understand it more. I started to look at what transpired not as a loss but rather a rescue. I know, you are saying "what"! Let me explain. God is controlling my life and that does not mean that He sends trouble like this but it does mean He allowed it to happen. I fully believe that there was enough power within our family to survive that hit and we could have come though this storm intact and stronger.

But WE both would have had to be in that same place and we were not. My survival and future were contingent on allowing God to do what He wanted through me. And I had to release my heart to allow Him to do that for my life partner, too. Starting to believe that He was steering me in a different direction (apart from her) and allowing myself to leave the shore and sail again was very difficult. I kept wanting to go back and rescue <u>her</u> and all the time He wanted to rescue <u>us</u>. You see it wasn't all about me and it wasn't all about her. It wasn't even all about us. It was about our relationship with Him! I know that type of thinking may be radical for some of you. But you will have a very hard time healing and becoming complete in every area of your life if you look at your transition as a loss or a theft. God is working in you and through you and taking you someplace different. Trust the journey. Trust the process. Trust Him!

The disciples had new surroundings all the time as they went out under the anointing and power that Jesus gave them. When you read verses 11-16 over again you will see that they had some guidance for how to approach where to go, what to do when they arrived and how to leave. Most people that go through transitions have the greatest difficulty in the last part...how to leave. When God tells you that its time to change jobs and you stay longer than you were supposed to, things may get very difficult before you leave. The longer you stay where you are not supposed to be the harder it will be to leave. I often wonder why He seems to move us when things are somewhat comfortable and going quite well right where we are. I don't like to move. But I never want to stay anywhere longer than I am supposed to. I realized that when I first became restless in my job in the Christian music industry. If I were honest with myself and with my hindsight being 20/20, I would have to say that the Lord was prompting me to make a change 5 years before I actually made the decision. Those final five years were not the most blessed, they were the most difficult. Perhaps because I stayed longer than I was supposed to. Maybe I stopped listening and started staying busy thinking about how to make the restlessness go away? Whatever, when it came time to leave I wanted to do so with a measure of grace and class. I never want to burn bridges because as they say, you may have to pass over them again later! Don't stir up a storm and animosity when it is time to go, just go. He told the disciples to respect each home, bless that home, and let your peace rest upon it. If they are receptive, let peace and blessing rule. If they are not receptive, well the instructions are much different. Look at what He told them. Shake the dust off of your feet when you leave.

There is a graceful way to leave the things that God is allowing to take place in your life. You will only be responsible for your part in the equation. So it is very important to maintain integrity and always take the high road. When you have been at a job for a long time and that season is over and it is time to leave it will never be easy. But it can be life changing for good.

I believe that Jesus told the disciples to shake the dust of their feet as a symbolic way of moving forward. They were to leave the difficulties they had there, there. It was also to set them up for where they were going. Imagine getting to the next city or home and having the dirt from the previous one still on you. When you go to that new job and still have on you some of the dirt from the previous one, it damages you but also the new company you are being sent to. Relationships work the same way. Shake the dust off. Don't allow the residue of the past to make a mess in your present. That is a very easy thing to say and a difficult one to apply. There is something that makes us feel better when we are able to blame the past for why we are where we are. But remember, we are reframing our thinking! God is bringing you to where you are so you really don't have to blame anyone or anything anymore! You are right where you are supposed to be…in the middle of a beautiful and life changing transition!

Now I don't want you to think that you are just living carelessly and everything that happens is God and you simply whistle and hop down this transitional trail with no responsibility. You have a responsibility to yourself and those attached to you to be wise. Jesus said that we are to be shrewd as snakes and as harmless as doves. You are not a doormat! Don't let the world shake off its residue on you! Be wise and smart and take care of you and those closest to you. And do it in a dove-like manner. The dove represents the Holy Spirit…when Jesus was being baptized by John the Baptist and he came up out of the water, the Holy Spirit descended upon him like a dove and God announced how pleased He was with His son. Let the Holy Spirit guard you and guide you. You do not have the responsibility of cleaning off everyone else's shoes…all you need clean are yours.

You've heard many people say that when you change your thinking you can change your life. I would take that a step further and say that in order to truly change your life you have to activate that new thinking with steps towards your God-given dream. I know that we do not always have a clear picture but if we can start to walk in the right direction we will begin to see clearer and we begin to get nearer. As you read the other verses of chapter 10 you see that even when difficult times arrive and we are "held captive" by things beyond our control, God will give us the words to say. It won't be you speaking. It will be the Spirit of God that is working in you that guides your speech and your steps.

Are you still carrying the "dirty" residue from your last location on your shoes? Perhaps today, through the anointing that God has given you and by the power of His Spirit, you can shake it off!

Chapter 18

I would imagine that one of the greatest and most significant crossing over experiences is from life to death. This is one that everybody gets to experience first hand. In the local newspaper it often refers to these experiences under a caption called, what else, TRANSITIONS. This is one transition that most certainly we are not prepared for and most often do not know is coming. Though we may not be prepared and even surprised by its arrival, it arrives just the same. And unless you have had the chance to personally talk to someone that has crossed over and returned back, we may never know how we will deal with this one.

I sort of believe that this particular transition is harder to watch than it is to go through. As part of my role as a pastor I have had to be with many people that watch a loved one cross over. The final moments of life in this mortal body are very difficult to witness because it methodically shuts down as if it was given an internal system to shut off when its life was finished. On the ones that I have witnessed it appears to be organized and calculated when it happens.

The uniqueness of this transition is that while the party passing is on theirs, the ones left behind begin theirs too. Comfort is what we want but these kinds of things are never comfort-able. One of my most difficult seasons in dealing with death came while I was working as the Executive Director of Carman Ministries. I had a wonderful, intelligent lady named Lisa that worked with me. She enabled me to do many things at once because she was so sharp. She was helping Carman and me with all of the administrative tasks that had to be done. And she was great. She and her husband had been trying to have a child and while she was working with us she got pregnant. Once she found out she was the happiest person on the planet. You could hear it in her voice and see it in her eyes. She had prepared for this and desired this all of her life and now her moment was here. Fast forward to the trip to the hospital, and the birthing process—the enthusiasm and excitement never left. In fact it increased. Suddenly, something went wrong with her blood cell count and while they were delivering her child she had complications. I was at the hospital with

her family and many of her friends and I was praying
with all that was in me for her to be fine. But it
never happened. She gave birth to a precious baby
boy and the Lord took her home. What that left,
besides a void in all of those closest to her, was a
plethora of people going through a variety of transitions. The parents were watching their daughter
pass, Lisa's husband was welcoming his first born
son, friends were dealing with her sudden departure
and I was feeling so confused. Life taken away, new
life coming in. I asked all of the questions that most
people do...why Lord? Why now? She always
wanted this and she had lived her entire life for this
moment...why was it happening like this? For three
days I sat in the office she used to occupy and questioned the Lord. I questioned what I was doing
because we had prayed and I wanted her to live. She
wanted to live.

You see many things happen that are simply
outside of our control zone. Many are the plans in a
man's heart but it is the Lords purpose that will
prevail. Trying to understand His purpose is the
journey of every believer. There have been stories
about people that came back. They all seem to have
a common thread of seeing bright light and feeling
beautiful sensations...that is if they are saved.

Those that do not know Christ have talked about tormenting screams and darkness in their transition.

What really happens we will not ever truly know until we experience it for ourselves. But we do have some hope. It came to us as a gift from God and once fulfilled it gave us a seamless transition. The most significant life to death to life experience is the one that scripture tells us in the story of Jesus. For three days he appeared to be dead. He had been brutalized, crucified and hung on a cross as payment for the sins of mankind. But death had to be defeated. The grave had to lose its sting. On the morning of the third day the tomb was empty and the stone that protected it had been rolled away though it had been guarded by soldiers. It was miraculous and it was supernatural. It's not just history, its HIS-story. It was God's plan for paying the price for each one of us so that there would no longer be a life to death transition without the possibility of eternal life in Christ. Scripture tells us that when we are "born-again", that means when we have asked Christ to be Lord of our lives, we are made new and our old sinful nature is dead. Our new spiritual man is alive and when we allow that spirit to guide us, we know that once we cross-over from this world we step into the eternity that has been promised to us in His word. As I said it is seamless, effortless and is one that we do not have to fear but should live life prepared so that we can embrace it. You see all of these other transitions, single to married, no children to children, unemployed to employed etc. ; these all seem insignificant when compared to our passage to the other side into eternity.

Where do you line up where Jesus is concerned? Many folks have walked away from "religion" and in doing so have missed the <u>relationship</u> that is theirs for the asking. The lady with the issue of blood that had been sick for 12 years just had to touch Him with her belief to be well. The disciples had to make room in their boat for Him to weather the storm and get to the other side of the lake. What do you need to do? I urge you today, to activate His purpose and plan for your life and ASK Him to live in your heart and through your life right now. It will make all the difference in this world and the world to come!

Chapter 19

There are a group of folks out there that are bold, faithful, and ready to die for this country. Some call them the few, the proud. Others call them an army of one. They are the men and women of our armed forces. Many of them were just kids when the Vietnam War took place or the war in Korea. Even with Desert Storm and now Iraq it is often kids that are placed in war zones. Add to that fathers and mothers, sons and daughters, grandkids and you have a lot of transitioning taking place. We call it being deployed which is just a fancy way to say they are leaving home and their return is uncertain. They are going from being civilians to soldiers with very little prep time considering what they will face. And their families are going from stable and thriving to unstable and surviving in a matter of days and weeks.

We have all seen and heard the stories of these heroes and how they endure their warfare season. Some return and some do not but all are heroes.

Another issue arrives for many of those that returned and came back from a war as a child, dealing with what they witnessed and experienced now as adults. Reliving the moment they took a life or engaged in a struggle. Watching a friend die in their arms or losing a limb. All real life happenings with unreal consequences. How do you handle this journey and make it to the other side of the war? Your body has come back but your mind is still there. I think of that man at the pool of Bethesda in John 5 that we talked about in an earlier chapter. His mind was there by the healing pool but his body was not. And because of his condition he had no way to get well. Or so we thought.

In walked the answer. Not dispensing healing but asking questions. Why? Because you and I have to want to get well to be able to get well. The first step toward solving a problem is to admit you have one. Often the trouble lies dormant for years and never changes. Then one day a situation, a conversation, an event triggers it into a living force that must be reckoned with. If we never answer the question, we may never see the complete healing that is already ours IN Christ.

TRANSITIONS

My mom's brothers served our country in Vietnam. They have been through a multitude of transitions, many that we are discussing in this book. Her youngest brother, John, like me is a single father having weathered divorce. He has been a very successful principal in the educational system and now works at a golf club and having the time of his life. After many years, suddenly he is now walking into that arena where all of us begin to face our own mortality. We are seeking a deeper meaning for why we are on the planet and asking if all of our decisions were the best ones and will our children be alright. In this season of exploration, the time spent in Vietnam has risen to the surface. Now face to face with those battle scenes, he is trying to transition completely to the other side in body and in mind. Here is his story...

I was 19 years old and a happy-go-lucky kid who had a great life. Unexpectedly, in the summer of 1966, having been drafted, I found myself in the Army. After six months of basic and advanced training, I received orders to APO San Francisco, which meant Vietnam. One of the most difficult things in leaving home was saying goodbye to my Mom and Dad. I have never seen them cry that hard in my life. In fact, until my departure for southeast Asia, I had never seen my father cry at all. I arrived in Ben Hoa Airbase waiting assignment to a replacement unit. I was assigned to the 9th Infantry Division 3/5 Cavalry Unit. After one week of in country training, I was sent out to the jungle. There is no way I was prepared for what the next year of my life would be.

The first few weeks were free of fear but veteran status took over very soon. You took one day at a time, knowing that each day puts you one day closer to going home. I guess surviving was always on your mind, but during firefights you really didn't think about that. You just did what you had to do.

Since I am writing this, I did survive. When I returned to the U.S. I did have a different attitude towards life. There is nothing life or death here and I have lived that philosophy my entire life since Vietnam. After marriage, kids, a divorce, and retirement, I was in my early 50's and something started bothering me. I had taken lives in Vietnam and killing was wrong. I had taken a retirement job at a golf course and a Catholic priest would stop by to visit my boss. One afternoon, Father St. Marie and I started talking. I was raised a Catholic but had been away from the church for a long, long time. We carried on these casual conversations for about two years. I finally opened up to him about my feelings regarding my Vietnam experience. He invited me to his church and absolved me of my concerns. I am happy to say that I have transitioned back to my church and feel that this priest somehow rescued me.

My Uncle, John Laslo

You will always come across people that help steer you back on course when you keep moving forward in God. You will find out some powerful things about yourself as my Uncle John did. God uses people to get you on track and keep you on track. Civilian life to being a soldier and then back to civilian again is quite a transition experience. My mom's other brother also served our country. He faced some interesting circumstances as he transitioned from war to home. I am sure he could write his own book. Here's part of his story…

I departed for Vietnam in August 1967 after going through several preparatory training periods. I was scheduled to command an Infantry Company in the First Cavalry Division in Vietnam (even though I was an Armor Officer) under a program the Army called Program Infusion. I was a Captain at the time and actually looked forward to my pending assignment.

TRANSITIONS

My tour could have easily been divided in two parts – before and after TET 68. Prior to TET 68, it seemed as though we would go through the motions but lacked the ambition to engage in serious combat with the Viet Cong (VC), our adversary in the Mekong Delta. After TET 68, and the devastation caused by both the VC and the North Vietnamese Army (NVA) and their attacks on District and Province Capitals as well as military installations, the conflict took on a more serious attitude. I was lucky, survived several near misses and lost a couple of close friends who were members of my Advisory Team. I remember advice I received from another senior officer – STAY ALERT STAY ALIVE. I never forgot that advice and practiced it constantly. I was consistently conscious of the wife and three children I had left in Columbus, GA and my actions, though professional and tactically correct, were taken with them in mind. I had prepared myself for combat and many of my actions were instinctive and appropriate for the combat situation.

My return home was eagerly awaited and when it came I was able to arrange a helicopter ride to Saigon, and was relieved when my plane lifted off of Than Son Nhut Air Force Base for my return home. After a quick stop at Hawaii for refueling, we finally

*landed at Travis AFB in Oakland, CA. We were
advised before leaving Vietnam not to travel in military uniform in the states because of the anti-war
protesters that were everywhere. I had my wife
Martha send me a couple of items of civilian attire
which I changed into in a restroom upon my arrival
at the San Francisco Airport. I still had very short
hair, was wearing Army jungle boots and carrying a
duffle bag which attracted a couple of "misfits" in
the terminal. They came at me, yelling and cursing,
and I kept walking. I stopped when one spit on me
and we went at it for a brief moment until some
security personnel jumped in and kept us apart.
"Welcome Home!" Martha was there at the terminal in Columbus, GA. to meet me when I arrived.
She ran to me and we held on to each other for quite
a while. The kids were not with her and I didn't get
to see them until I arrived back at the house. Boy,
had they grown in the 13 months that I was gone.
They ran to meet the car as we arrived in the drive-
way and for the next several hours we hugged,
talked and thanked God for my safe return home.
For the next 30 days we got to know each other
again, spent a lot of time talking about what had
happened while I was gone and made plans for our
move from Columbus to Fort Leavenworth, Kansas,*

my next assignment. That kept us pretty busy and it was strange but reassuring to be able to sleep through a quiet night without gunfire and explosions and to lay on a soft warm bed next to a lady I dearly loved. I did have a couple of bad nights and sat in the dark thinking about what I had experienced, the incidents that could have turned out different save for a short span of time or space, and what I could have done different to effect a more positive outcome. These were sort of "lessons learned" episodes that took several months to completely divorce from my mind.

Martha and the kids did everything they could to make my homecoming a special time for us all. They made extensive plans for my return and laid out several things to do and places to go when I returned. They didn't give me much time to brood over my experience. They didn't pressure me to talk about Vietnam and that was fine with me. We had exchanged several letters while I was gone and I even purchased a couple of small recorders that we used to send messages back and forth which allowed us to frequently hear each other's voices. This frequent contact made my return home easier and prevented me from becoming a stranger while I was gone. I believe the secret to making the transition back to the family was frequent contact during the absence, doing things as a family to keep from thinking about what I had left behind in Vietnam, and most of all just staying busy. Lastly, as was my habit, I focused on the future and not on the past. It was simply great to be home where I belonged.

My Uncle Col. George Laslo

That story really bring out Paul's words in Philippians 3:13, "forgetting those things that are behind and straining towards what is AHEAD..." Uncle George was looking ahead.

We must never ever forget what those brave souls have done to fight for the freedom that we enjoy in this country. Freedom comes with a price. Freedom also brings transition...from being captive to being free. May God bless the men and women of our armed forces, their families and the lives that they change each and every day with their service.

Chapter 20

TRANSITIONS...can't live with them, can't live without them...but you can live through them! The common thread that runs through every transition that is endured is the help of a higher power...someone or something bigger than ourselves. I found that in Jesus Christ when I made him Lord of my life in 1977 in a dorm room at the University of Cincinnati. And because He is my Savior and Lord today I realize that when I look at all of the transitions in life, LIFE itself is a transition. Imagine that, I have a number of years to endure this one before I cross over to the other side and live for eternity with Christ.

I want to invest my time wisely because I do not know when my parking permit will be validated and I will be called home. I will be moved from one position to the next in many ways for the duration of my stay here and I know that I am only passing through. Though life gets muddy sometimes and that dirt clouds our thinking and our vision, life in

Christ can wash away the dirt and allow us to see more clearly than we have ever seen before. I can be baptized out of the "stuff" and into the wonderful and marvelous things that have been planned out for me while I am here. It makes me think of my annual vacation with my parents. Each year my brother and sister and their families meet my mom and dad at a chosen destination. We know that we will only have about a week together and that being the case, my mom (Nana to the kids), has an agenda that she and dad (aka-Pop) have laid out. Each day has a major event and some minor ones sprinkled in too. But you know the greatest part. Though they would like us to do everything, though they really want all of the grandkids to do all of the incredible stuff, they allow us to choose what we want to do. And some of us "lazy" ones choose to stay home while others go on the exciting expedition in search of stars and living creatures!

You know God has a wonderful plan for you too. He really wants you to do all of the great activities that He has planned out for your days and he would love to see you do them with a cheerful heart and a smile. He presents the opportunities, the daily schedule, and then just like good ole Nana and Pop, He lets us choose. There have not been many things that I chose not to do on our vacations that I regretted. And you know what, I can't go back and do them. I can only pray that I never do the same thing in my life that I sometimes do on my vacation. It was Robert Frost that said,

"I will pass this way but once.
And if there's any good that I can do,
let me do it now"

Now is good. When I turn NOW around I WON! Life is short and time is fleeting. This transition will not last forever. Just like all of the others that life surrounds us with, this too will pass. What are you doing with your life? If you don't do something with life, life will do something with you. Let me suggest a plan...do something great! Make it big, so big that unless God helps you it could never be done! Your going to dream anyway so why not dream BIG...not 5 X 7 or 8 X 10...lets keep enlarging the image! With God ALL things are possible and you are crossing over in a BIG way!

Remember we are all just REAL people with
REAL problems, looking for REAL answers
which can only be found in a very REAL God!

Add Your Own
TRANSITION stories here!

_____

_____

_____

_____

_____

_____

_____

_____

_____

_____

_____

_____

_____

_____

_____

_____

_____

_____

_____

_____

_____

_____

TRANSITIONS

TRANSITIONS

TRANSITIONS

TRANSITIONS

LaVergne, TN USA
21 May 2010
183484LV00001B/1/P